Published in February 2011 by:
SkyVault™ Multimedia Publishing Group
Edited by Ashtay Productions
888-461-0734

DISCLAIMER AND/OR LEGAL NOTICES:

While all attempts have been made to verify information provided in this publication, neither the Author nor the Publisher assume any responsibility for errors, inaccuracies, or omissions. Any slights of people or organizations are unintentional.

I HATE MY LIFE:
A TEENAGER'S STORY

EARLY BEGINNING

It seems like pain has been my partner from the beginning. My mom only carried me for 7 months; but what a long, terrible 7-

month pregnancy it was for both of us.

Unfortunately, my mom endured a lot of verbal abuse and stress from my dad while she carried me. He was not a compassionate or understanding man. The pregnancy even ended stressfully – when I was being born, the umbilical cord got wrapped so tight around my neck that I almost didn't get here alive.

As I grew up, the arguing and fighting between my parents continued. My mom would always say "please don't argue in front of the children", but my dad wasn't hearing it. He always had to have the last word, and things always went his way. My mom went to a shelter several times just to get away from his abuse.

Although mom hated the shelter, she hoped that he would miss us and that this would make him change. But the fighting just went on and on. The first

time I saw my dad hit my mom was on the way to church one Sunday morning. In fact, they were arguing about me. My dad did not like what I had on, so he hit my mom in the eye with his fist.

My mom was always working. But when she got home, she would cook, clean, help us with our homework, and still make some play

4

time with us. We would sing, she would hold us and kiss us. Boy, how I missed my mom during the day.

I remember having a dream about my dad holding a gun to my head and threatening my mom. It really scared me. I told my mom, and she said she was sorry I had such a bad dream. Later on she told me that she had the same dream and that she was afraid. She said that one day she was going to leave for good and would take us with her.

I looked forward to that day, because mom always looked after us better than dad did. When my mom would work late, my dad would give us a sandwich or cereal instead of a meal. He never played with us. He would just come home from work, watch television, and go to sleep.

One day my mom decided to leave again. She

5

tried to take us with her but my dad kept us behind him so she could not reach us. My mom did not want to get hit again, so she left in tears. I had seen my mom get hit before, so I'm sure she did not want to get hit again.

My dad told us that my mom went to court and they said he had to let her have visits with us. Sometimes he would let her visit, and sometimes he wouldn't. My mom would cry and beg him to let her see us. I remember him making us run upstairs just so we couldn't leave with our mom.

I also remember him telling us when we visited the church my mom attended, that we better not take communion. He told us she was going to Hell, and we better not participate in anything at her church.

When I look back, it seems like my parents argued over everything. I remember being in first grade and my dad made my bath water but it was much too hot. I screamed, but he said to shut up. My mom ran in and told him to add cold water to it, but was told to shut up and mind her own business. So the arguing began.

During one visit, my mom noticed corns on my feet. She cried because she knew I got them because my shoes were too small. She didn't want to fight with dad about it, so she took me out to get new shoes even though I knew she couldn't afford to.

I loved my mom and I missed her so much. I hated not being able to see her every day. My mom always showed me love and kindness. She played with us, and she would always be singing. When we did visit with our mom we had a great time. My mom, my sister and I would go to the park, then to the mall, and then have dinner. We never wanted the visits to end.

I remember one day crying and screaming because I did not want to go back home to my dad. My mom called the police to report my unhappiness about going back. The police did a report but told me I had to go back to my dad anyway. I cried louder and louder but it did not make a difference. I heard the police tell my mom that if my dad and her kept arguing about me, that I would end up in the system.

As the days, weeks, and months went by so did my unhappiness with living with my dad. He never wanted me or my sister to see our mom, and we couldn't talk to her on the telephone either. I felt so alone and lost without the affection my mom showed me.

I never felt any kindness when I was with my dad. When my mom told me she was going back to court so that she would be able to see us on a regular basis, I jumped for joy. I was so happy to hear this. Eventually my mom did get visitation, but my dad still made it difficult for her to see us on a regular basis.

I was very angry whenever I couldn't see my mom. My mom was fun to be with and made sure we had a good time. My dad had no interest in anything like that. I can remember my dad making us lie to our mom, even telling us to hide when she would come to see us. Every time it happened, it tore me up inside.

CHILDHOOD

One day my dad started packing and he told us we were moving "back home to Florida". On the way there, the police stopped my dad and made him pull over. I did not know what was going on. Later they took my dad to  jail. We waited in the lobby for a long time. A day or so later, we were released back to our dad and we continued on with our trip.

Several months went by, and I wondered if and when I would ever see my mom again. Then one day it happened; she appeared, and I was so happy I couldn't believe it. The last time I had seen my mom, I was in New Jersey. Now I was in Florida - how did she find me? I was in school, and it was such a wonderful surprise.

I ran to my mom and hugged her so tight. My mom could not decide if she should go by my dad's place and get our clothes and things or just take us home with her. My sister said, "let's go get your things". My mom said, "No, I'd better not. I don't want any problems with your dad". I said, "Yeah mom, let's just go home with you". And we left to go home.

I later asked my mom how she found us. She said she went to the judge and got the papers reviewed and he gave custody to her. I said "Good mom, "cause I don't like living with dad".

As I started to live with my mom, I was so happy. Life was great! Unfortunately, it did not last long. My dad started taking my mom to court to fight over the custody papers. It wasn't long before I was back living with him. I cried, screamed, and fought hard not to go back with him. I even spoke to a case worker to tell him how I felt. I guess it didn't matter because I'm a kid and they think I don't know what is right or wrong.

Being back with my dad was unbearable. I could not believe tragedy was hitting me again. Unhappy days and nights were once again a part of my life. I didn't care anymore about anything. I didn't get my school work done, and I didn't play anymore with anyone. I was very unhappy. Some friends at school tried to console me, but it didn't work.

Sometimes, when my dad would keep mom from seeing us on her visitation days, she would come to church and sit by me. I was so happy to see her. When my dad found out that she was sitting by me, he would get angry and snatch me up and throw me in the car. He would then argue with my mom about coming to see me. I was upset that my dad would keep me from being with my mom.   I missed her so much.

When we got home, he would beat me for letting her sit by me. I was angry with my dad for beating me and putting marks on me again. I was also embarrassed because the people in church saw it. I knew mom was hoping my dad would finally cooperate and let her see me, but he never did. I knew my mom was hurt and disappointed.

One day my dad beat me pretty bad for not doing my homework, and he put me on punishment.   He even locked me in the house while he went out on a date with his girlfriend. I remember being so hungry while he was gone; he told me not to touch anything or he would beat me again.   But I was hungry and scared. What should I do?

One night I sneaked and called my mom.   I was so happy that she was home.   I was so hungry and lonely. She consoled me, and we talked past midnight. I told her I was hungry but dad said not to eat anything while he was gone, and I did not want to get another beating.

She said to fix me a peanut butter and jelly sandwich and clean up real good after myself and then he won't know. I was so scared to do this, because I didn't want my dad to beat me again. I already had marks on my legs and they looked bad. My mom kept trying to tell me it would be ok. I remember asking her to send me a pop tart in the mail.

Every Friday night, I would call my mom and we would talk. She told me how much she loved me and that she missed me a whole lot. I even prayed to God to please help my mom get custody of me. I promised to be a good boy. I just wanted to be happy and live with my mom.

She also said that she would continue to fight to get me back. This gave me so much comfort. My mom said it hurt her to know that I was hungry, alone, and afraid of getting beatings. She said we had to stop talking like this and do something about it.

She told me to write a note saying I'm hungry and home alone on Friday nights. She said no one would believe her unless she had something from me in writing. So I did. I think I was around 10 years old. I didn't know if writing a note would really help, but I would do anything to be with my mom. She was there for me, and it helped me get through the long nights.   Thank you Lord for my mom. I miss her so much!

THE PRE-TEEN YEARS

Eventually, my mom was able to get visitation rights back. It was so good to be with mom, to feel relief from all the anxiety, fear, and beatings. During one visit, I told my mom, "I hate my life"! She was shocked.

"Why do you say that?" she asked. I told her it was because daddy beats me all the time.

I even showed her the marks. "I hate living with him." I even told one of my teachers, but nothing happened. I guess it's because I'm a kid – it's not important enough for anyone to care."

My mom said, "It saddens and hurts me

16

that you feel this way. No child should have to feel this way or go through such sadness." She went on to say that she would continue to fight for me, and I knew she would. I really enjoyed the weekends with my mom. She would always listen, and she was always fun. I knew my mom loved me. When it was time to go back to my dad, we both cried. My mom was shaking and holding me.

I remember being sad and angry a lot in school. My spirit was in pain all the time. I never laughed or had fun like the other kids, and I had no one to play with at home. Not that my dad ever allowed any play time anyway.

I couldn't understand why life was so hard for me. "Why can't I stay with my mom?" I would ask, but I would never get a decent answer.

My sister and I both hated living with my dad. When I was 9, we ran away from home.

17

Unfortunately, he caught us and made us go back. A year later, my sister left for good and was able to stay with my mom. I never did understand why I couldn't go too. Life for me was so sad and dark. All I wanted was to get away from my dad. I didn't want to have to face the gloom of everyday life anymore. "God please help me"!

One day, some guys at school asked me if I wanted to smoke a cigarette. I said no, but eventually I tried it, and learned to like it. Later they introduced me to marijuana, and I learned to like that too. It made me forget about the constant sadness and pain I was feeling all the time.

Then one beautiful day, my mom came and got me. It was the middle of the week, and I just happened to be outside when she came. She said it had been a long and expensive fight, but she was finally there to take me back once and for all.

I couldn't believe it - my dream had finally come true! I couldn't stop hugging and kissing her. I finally had a clean house to live in, plenty of good food, laughter, and fun with my sister and mom. Oh, thank you God!

I loved living with my mom. I was so happy. It was a whole new wonderful world for me. I remember my mom was in a car accident. She was hurt pretty bad. My sister and I was there for her to help her walk, go to the grocery store, and help clean up. I was glad to help my mom and to be there for her.

Unfortunately, a couple of months later, I met this boy who lived in the complex next to ours and I started doing the things that he did. I don't know why I was so influenced by him. Sometimes I think I was just bored, and it was just nice to finally have someone to play with. Maybe it was because we did things - exciting things that I never even knew about before. We sprayed the walls with black paint. We skipped school. He even convinced me to take my mom's car and go joyriding. I knew it was wrong, but he told me she wouldn't know about it because we would only be gone for a few minutes.

He was right. We got away with it, so we did it again. We kept doing it until we had an accident with her car. My friend had asked me to try a different kind of weed that he had, and I did. I was so high, I couldn't see good, so I let my friend drive. Wrong move. The guy hit a pole, and I knew I was in trouble. My mom was so angry and upset with me over getting her new car wrecked.

At first I lied, but later I told her the truth. My mom was in tears. Skipping school was bad enough, but to wreck her car was too much. She said this was a hard decision for her to make, but she wanted me to learn a lesson.

20

She decided to have me go into a program to help me with my behavior choices and the decisions that I make.

I felt so bad that I hurt my mom. I didn't like the program, but I went anyway. Later, I was happy that I did because the guy I was with kept getting into trouble and ended up going to juvenile detention. I did not want to end up there.

THE TEENAGE YEARS

As time went on, I met some other guys in the complex where I lived. I started hanging with them and things seemed good. It wasn't long before they started  asking me about my mom. They wanted to come over.

They had been watching my mom and knew her work schedule. They also knew when we went to church, and that I was home by myself on Wednesday nights. I was supposed to go to church also, but sometimes my mom couldn't find me. Anyway, I thought it would be ok since we weren't doing

22

anything wrong. But things changed when they wanted to bring a drink with them while my mom was gone to church.

I remember one Wednesday night they called the pizza man over for a delivery. The plan was to rob him once he got inside. I was so scared.

Things didn't quite go according to plan. The delivery man came in, but he had no money on him. The guys beat him up because they wanted money and were mad that he didn't have any.

When my mom came home, she was furious! She could not believe that such a scheme had taken place in her home. She was very relieved that the man did not get robbed, but upset that he got beat up. So she put me on punishment and refused to compromise.

I don't know why I let other people talk me into doing dumb things. I wanted to do better, but as time went on, I always seemed to find myself back on the wrong path.

I was getting more and more out of control. My mom couldn't do anything with me. Even though my world had finally changed for the better, for some reason I hadn't. I was always angry, always sad. I never smiled or laughed, and I stopped talking with my mom.

I don't know why I was this way. I lost interest in schoolwork, and started having behavior and anger problems all the time. I couldn't seem to help myself. I still felt miserable, and I took it out on my teacher and my mom.

Things got so bad, my mom took me to a friend's house in another city for her to keep me. My mom would come every week to

24

bring money and to check on me.

Things were ok there, but I still wasn't happy, and the lady that was keeping me was having some personal difficulties of her own. I also got into a car accident while I was living with her. Wow, this was not fun.
Eventually, mom brought me back home again. I went back to my old ways and started smoking weed more often.

I really don't know why, but I was always being angry and mean towards my sister. I do know that somewhere deep inside, I was angry that she got to live with mom before I did. I hated that I got left behind to live with dad.

I just couldn't shake the anger. As I continued to do wrong, I became more withdrawn from my mom. One day I was so upset, I told her "I wanted to kill myself". I just couldn't understand life.

My mom took me to counseling, but it didn't help. The doctor couldn't help me solve my problems. All he wanted to do was prescribe medication for me. I hated taking pills.

One day, before my counseling session, I tore up the waiting area. The doctor was afraid of me. My mom was upset, and I'll never forget the helpless look on her face.

Life had become a nightmare, for my mom and for me. I had no idea things would go so badly. One day I asked her, "mom, why did we have to have a dysfunctional life?"

She said, "I didn't want our lives to be this way. I have tried to make a happy home for all of us."
I knew she was right. But for some reason, I still couldn't escape the sense of misery and sadness I felt all the time.

One summer day, my mom and I were out walking in the park. Somehow we started talking about drugs. She said, "promise me you will not use drugs or sell them." She had been saying this to me since I was a little boy, so it was not a new request.

I admitted to her that I was already using drugs, but promised I would never use crack.

My mom had me admitted to special programs, and I had to go to special schools. Nothing helped. One day I did use crack, and shortly afterwards I started selling it. Of course, I wound up going to jail.

I tried to do better when I got out, but by this time, my mom had put me out of the house. She was very upset and angry with me. I had put her through too much. She was showing me that she would not continue to go through crazy and unnecessary changes with me any

27

longer. I guess I had disappointed and hurt her too many times. So I slept in the park near our home, or in empty houses that I could find. I had no appetite, and I lost weight until I was no bigger than a tooth pick. I could feel my life spiraling down, and I couldn't stop it. "Lord help me please! I'm so messed up. I never thought my life would be so horrible.

I found myself thinking once again, "I hate my life".

ADULT LIFE

For some reason I could not pick myself up and go the right way. There just didn't seem to be any good reason to. So I continued to use drugs and sell them as well. I bought cars,  clothes, and dated lots of girls.

I was making plenty of money, but I knew I was living on the edge, and I had to be very careful. It was nowhere near as much fun as it sounds. I did not finish high school, I stayed angry, and I still didn't know what to do with my life.

Sometimes I would cry when I thought about all the times I disappointed my mom, and caused her to cry. I felt so bad when I thought about the times I stole other people cars or personal items. Why did my life have to be so crazy? Why couldn't I be like other boys?

Sometimes I would talk to God and ask Him to help me get myself together. I have been to jail so many times now. I have missed 4 birthdays in detention or jail. I have also missed Christmases and other holidays by being locked up.   Most of the time, I just felt lost.

As time went on, my behavior got more and more reckless. I was so far out there, but I didn't know how to stop. One day I was riding with a friend, on our way to get some drugs. After we got the stuff, the police stopped us.

 As they approached the car, I ran and hid at another friend's house. But they brought dogs in, and they caught me. I ended up in jail again, and this time it was serious. I was looking at prison time. Man, I couldn't believe I'd been so stupid. This was not a good day for me at all.

On visiting day, my mom would come to see me. On one particular visit I told her, "Mom, I was waiting for the right time to tell you this, but now is as good as any - I got a girl pregnant."

She said, "I hope the baby is healthy."

I said, "Mom, if I go up the river, would you please look out for my child? Promise me, mom."

She said, "Of course I will. I'll take pictures and send them to you, as well as videotape the moments you don't want to miss out on."

I'm hoping you don't go to prison", she continued. "I will do all I can to keep you from having to go that route. I don't know how

31

much I can do since I don't have any money, but perhaps I can use the home as loan collateral. We'll see."

Well, mom did try, but unfortunately nothing worked. I was sentenced to prison. The state wanted seven years, but I ended up getting three and a half due to the mental evaluations that had been done, and because I had been going from home to home. It was a break, but I certainly didn't feel happy. I was scared, I was hurt, and I was asking God to help me. I hated jail - how could I survive in prison?

CONCLUSION

As I sit in my cell, watching my life slowly pass me by, I think about my mom a lot. I remember one day when we were talking, she said I had an anger problem. I always denied it. But now, years later, I can see it clearly.

The last time she came to visit I admitted to her, "You're right, mom. I do have an anger problem. I get angry very easily, I realize that now."

So many times, I wish I had a better life, a normal life. So many times, I also wish I had

33

listened to my mom. I hate my life the way it is now, but I recognize that there are choices within my control that can make things better. I am praying that I get it right when I am released from prison.

The purpose of this book is to let parents - especially young parents - know that it is so important how you treat a child while they are growing up. It's important that you know that fighting in front of a child is very damaging. It promotes a lot of anger, low self-esteem and fear.

It's also damaging to live with an abusive parent. Had my dad not been abusive to my mom, we wouldn't have had to leave our home to go stay in emergency shelters.

My mom would not have been stressed out and unhappy during her pregnancy, which caused me to move around too much and get the umbilical cord wrapped around my neck before I was born.

My dad made our whole family miserable. We suffered because of him.

So my advice is for you to be very, very selective about who you decide to have a child with. Turmoil, separation, and divorce significantly affects a child – in lots of ways that nobody seems to really understand.

Life is a lot harder without both parents. It's hard not to be able to talk to them. It's hard to keep your feelings locked up all the time. It affects who you are. It changes you as a person. And it causes a child to have a miserable life.

The bottom line is, you can't count on the system to correct your mistakes. The lawyers, judges, c o unselors and case workers aren't really interested in finding the right solution to your problems; they just want a fast solution that gets you out of their hair and off of their caseload.

A teacher might take a genuine interest, but they don't have time to be everybody's parents. Most of them already have too many students to look after - and perhaps kids of their own they're trying to raise.

I would not want any child to live like I did. The Hell I went through could have been prevented if I had a loving and kind father. I see now how mental and physical abuse can ruin your life.

I could not handle all the anger that was built up inside me. My mom never had a chance in saving me. By the time she finally got custody of me, it was too late. Too much damage had been done, and I was already in a mindset to start making bad choices.

I now realize that I have a depression problem, an anger problem, and a drug problem. The third one certainly doesn't help the other two, although I thought it would at first. That temporary good feeling is definitely not worth the new Hell I introduced into my life.

It's time I learned how to feel good without having to get high.

I am determined to work on all three of my challenges, and try to have a normal life when I get out. I am a father now. I want to be a good father to my son. I want him to have a happy childhood.

It's too bad I had to go to prison to finally turn to God for real, but now I pray to Him daily to send me the resources I need. I know now that He is the father who's always there to comfort and care for me. I can finally feel the blessings He's giving me and my family.

I didn't have the greatest dad in the world. But I was blessed with a fabulous mother. I am so happy that she and my sisters are still standing by me and helping to take care of my son while I've been gone.

My life can be an example for this young man-child, or a warning. I realize now that the choice is up to me.

Please learn from my mistakes.
Have a happy life. Love your life. God is blessing me greatly. May He bless you and your family as well.

Ladies and Gentlemen:

It's with great conviction that I write this letter about Ms. Linda Mobley.
In my role as Community Affairs Director for WFTS TV ABC Action News I oversee the station's annual domestic violence awareness campaign - Taking Action Against Domestic Violence Campaign

We first met Ms. Mobley in December 2011 at an event for CASA - the state certified domestic violence center serving Pinellas County. We were so impressed with the audience response to her play that we incorporated it into our domestic violence awareness campaign in 2012. Our studio interview with her was followed by a number if calls from parents, local advocates and even teachers asking for more information.

There is an over abundance of documents/ books/presentations for adults but items for teenagers are scarce.

We encourage you to take a closer look at Ms. Mobley's book - stage play "I Hate My Life". It may be exactly what your young audience needs to take positive steps towards healthy relationships.

Sincerely,
Lissette Campos
Director of Community Affairs
WFTS TV ABC Action News
(813) 354-2859
www.abcactionnews.com/dv

I am confident that Ms. Mobley's book has a role to play in the many discussions about family dynamics, peer influence and decision making skills that kids need to master in life. I am convinced that teenagers here in Pinellas County and throughout the nation can learn something of value by reading this book.

The readablilty of the book is on a grade level that the vast majority of our young kids can comprehend. The number of pages in the book is small but enough to capture the essence of the story.

I highly recommend Linda Mobley's book to be a fixture in all households, regardless of race and ethnicity.

Ray Tampa
Retired School Principal
Past NAACP President

Heat Stroke Management

How to Manage and Prevent Heat Stroke the Right Way

By
Paolo Jose de Luna

Paolo Jose De Luna

or abuse of any policies, processes, or directions contained within is the solitary and utter responsibility of the recipient reader. Under no circumstances will any legal responsibility or blame be held against the publisher for any reparation, damages, or monetary loss due to the information herein, either directly or indirectly.

Respective authors own all copyrights not held by the publisher.

The information herein is offered for informational purposes solely, and is universal as so. The presentation of the information is without contract or any type of guarantee assurance.

The trademarks that are used are without any consent, and the publication of the trademark is without permission or backing by the trademark owner. All trademarks and brands within this book are for clarifying purposes only and are the owned by the owners themselves, not affiliated with this document.